AFRICA'S LOST VINYL
RECORD PRESS

A TRUE STORY

GORDON WALLIS

Author's note: Some names have been
changed to protect the guilty.

TABLE OF CONTENTS

CHAPTER ONE: THE IDEA

I guess it was around early 2015. I was in my late forties and had lived in Harare, Zimbabwe all of my life. The economic decline of the Mugabe era had taken its toll on the country and my local businesses were suffering badly. Thankfully, I had been dealing in rare vinyl records on eBay for many years. Mainly Zimbabwean and South African pressings of Rock and Pop music. Both singles and albums. The demand for these exotic pressings was high when I first got started and there were many pleasant surprises along the way. Apart from the obvious artists like The Beatles, The Rolling Stones and Elvis Presley, I was amazed at the prices I was getting for the more obscure bands. It turned out that the Rhodesian/Zimbabwean pressing of 'God save The Queen' by The Sex Pistols was extremely rare and still is to this day, with the few copies that found their way onto the market realising many thousands of dollars. There were also rabid collectors of Iron Maiden, AC/DC, Deep Purple, The Cure, T-Rex, Metallica, Bob Dylan, U2, Kiss, Michael Jackson, Gary Numan, The Damned, Mike Oldfield, Bruce Springsteen, The Jam, even Dolly Parton and Olivia Newton John. I would find these old records at house sales, auction houses, and charity shops. I would then clean them up, take detailed photographs and list them on eBay. I can't tell you how many times I was approached by bidders wanting a 'Buy It Now' option. Occasionally I would agree but more often than not I would let the auction run its course. These auctions often ended in fierce bidding wars between collectors and realised very high prices indeed. A lot of these auction results can still be viewed on websites like Popsike and Collectors Frenzy.

After the auctions had ended and I was paid, I would pack the records into stiff cardboard sleeves and ship them worldwide from my local post office. The shipping usually took around two weeks and was, for the most part, reliable. Any record sold for over £50 was automatically sent via registered/signed for mail. The buyers were over the moon and I was earning a good living doing something I loved. I have been a music fan all my life and have been in several local rock bands over the years. The Zimbabwe Dollar had long since fallen into hyperinflation and obtaining hard currency was extremely difficult so I was onto a winner. Something I kept very close to my chest. The country was, and still is to some extent, under sanctions. Access to websites like Paypal was restricted so my finances accrued from vinyl sales were being handled by my Mother who lives in the UK. I would get remittances via Western Union or similar and sometimes from friends visiting from overseas who would bring cash. The Zimbabwean pressings of international bands were pressed in very small numbers, mainly for the relatively small local white population. Of course there were many local Shona and Ndebele bands pressed as well. These records, in all cases, had poor quality sleeves made from recycled board and the labels were no better, often with spelling and print errors. I guess for the serious collectors it was a case for ownership over quality, although as is the case with all rare vinyl, better quality resulted in better prices. Over the years I managed to buy large collections of albums and singles from DJs whose records had long been in storage since the advent of Compact Discs and electronic downloads. People saw no use in keeping them and quite often they were stored in garden sheds and were being damaged by termites and Cane Rats. In one case I bought a huge collection of DJ samples/promos from a person who had them stored in crates in his double garage. There were over ten thousand albums of all genres from the 1960s onwards, most with sample stamps to covers and labels. Some were from South Africa and had the banned tracks underlined to the rear of the sleeves with the word 'BANNED' written on Tippex as a warning to the DJs. The censorship boards in Rhodesia and South Africa were very touchy in the old days and tracks deemed to be inappropriate or risqué were immediately outlawed for airplay. Also included were a lot of old metal acetates from South Africa.

The huge collection of vinyl I had accumulated was starting to present a problem for me as far as storage was concerned. I had filled three large rooms with shelves and crates and had also built a large two room shed which I had permanently fumigated against the scourge of termites. Often working with slow and intermittent internet and poor cameras, I managed to upload roughly twenty records a day. I would schedule these auctions to run for a week and end at 9pm UK time to ensure my buyers were at home and ready to bid. Packing and shipping was usually done twice a week and I had many frustrating afternoons with my assistant, who was particularly careless in his sleeve-making and addressing skills. It was extremely annoying after all the effort I had put into describing the state of the vinyl and sleeves in such minute detail so as not to disappoint my buyers. Record collectors are a very fussy and unforgiving bunch! So for years my week days were spent like this and the evenings were spent watching my auctions end and invoicing the winning bidders. During the week I would also schedule a lot of auctions to end on Sunday evenings. This is a great time for auctions to end as most people are at home and relaxed. It would not be a good idea having a rare AC/DC record auction end say on a Friday or Saturday night. My thinking was most of the buyers would be out drinking and partying like other AC/DC fans. All of my auctions ended between Sundays and Thursdays. It was in this spirit that my own weekends were spent. And it was on a Saturday night at a party somewhere in Harare when a good friend of mine, Ralph Tatham, made a casual suggestion. As I spent so much time online I was more and more aware of the resurgence in the popularity of vinyl. Sales of new records were rising dramatically worldwide and it seemed to me that the trend would continue. Vinyl was back to stay. We were drinking and listening to music while I was telling him about recent vinyl sales.

"Gordy, why don't you find the machines that made those records and try to sell them?" he said. I thought about it briefly and told him I thought it was a good idea. I had no idea if the machines still existed or where they were. I also had no clue as to how the record manufacturing process was done. As the party was in full swing I decided to shelve the idea for another day. It was on a warm afternoon many months later that I remembered that conversation with Ralph and I decided to try and find Zimbabwe's lost vinyl record manufacturing plant.

CHAPTER TWO: THE HUNT

I knew from experience where to start. The various labels and sleeves on the Zimbabwe pressings were the clues. The Gallo label, the Gramma Records label, and the ZMC label which stood for Zimbabwe Music Corporation. Gallo and Gramma had become ZMC over the years as the company, and the country, changed names. The ZMC factory was, and still is, in the Msasa industrial site not far from my house. I had visited it on a few occasions looking for vinyl records. As a functioning company, it was struggling financially. Music piracy was a big problem for Zimbabwean artists and the advent of file sharing was not help-ing either. Beneath their offices and studios was a warehouse that sold locally produced CDs of Zimbabwean bands packed in cheap plastic sleeves. They also sold a variety of cassette tapes, some of which were by international acts like U2, Dolly Parton, and Elvis Presley. All of these were made by ZMC. I had sold a few of these over the years but they seemed more like items of curiosity to collectors. Vinyl records were what they *really* wanted. On one visit I got to meet the managing director of ZMC - a pleasant elderly man by the name of Emanuel Vori. We had spoken at length about the glory days of vinyl and he had told me many an entertaining story about local artists.

On one occasion I was invited to ZMC for an album launch by a famous Zimbabwean musician friend of mine, the late Andy Brown. I had also bought a large collection of vinyl albums from the personal collection of Mr Vori, so it was him who I called first. I was secretly hoping that the vinyl pressing plant was gathering dust in one of their warehouses but sadly this was not to be. It turned out that ZMC had sold the plant in the early 1990s to the Duke Box Music Company of Southerton, Harare. Once a huge concern with offices and employees countrywide, Duke Box had been around for many many years. As the name suggests, they used to own a substantial stock of vinyl jukeboxes and pinball machines. Thousands of these were scattered all over the country in the various clubs and pubs from the 1960s onwards until they became outdated and withdrawn. The company, although still based in their impressive factory in Southerton, had shrunk, and now mainly operated a few table football machines scattered around the capital. During that casual chat to Mr Vori I never asked him how much money Duke Box had paid for the record plant. I can only imagine it must have gone for a song. After all, at the time, the machines were defunct. Vinyl was dead and the future was all high tech.

After the phone call to Mr Vori I sat and thought about why Duke Box might have bought the plant in the first place. It puzzled me. I could only imagine that the reason was so they could continue producing singles for their many jukeboxes. However, at that time in 2015, I knew for sure that the jukeboxes no longer existed, at least not in public spaces. Perhaps they had scrapped the vinyl pressing plant? Broken the machines down and sold them for their weight in metal. Much later, I found out that this was exactly what EMI in the UK had done. I also later heard that the entire record pressing plant in South Africa had been taken out to sea and dumped overboard. This is hearsay, however, and I cannot verify that as fact. But this was not the only thing that worried me. I had heard about the owner of Duke Box Music, a certain Mr Slade Eatwell. He had inherited the business in his mid-fifties and his reputation preceded him. I had met him and his wife once at a restaurant in the city. The establishment was full at the time and we were stuck in the bar as we waited for our food. My girlfriend and I had struck up a conversation with him, and it had left us feeling cold. His wife was afraid of him. I had seen the grand Duke Box house on the Kariba Road heading out of Harare. I had once stayed at their company house on the Zambezi river at Chirundu whilst on a fishing trip with friends. They had told me in no uncertain terms that he was as mean as a snake. I decided to a bit more research before proceeding. I made a few phone calls to other friends to ask if they knew anything about him. Many of them did and the message was clear. The news was not good. By all accounts, he was a rather unpleasant man. Jealous, aggressive, and sneaky. Soon enough I would find out that they were 100% right. The man was a fucking asshole.

CHAPTER THREE: THE VISIT

Armed and primed with this information, I attempted to contact Mr Slade Eatwell. After numerous calls to the offices of Duke Box, I ascertained that he seldom visited his place of business. Many days later, after leaving numerous messages without reply, I managed to track him down on his mobile phone. I introduced myself and reminded him of the evening we had spent in the bar at the restaurant. I have no idea whether he remembered me or not. I did my best to sound cheerful and nonchalant as I enquired as to the existence and whereabouts of the plant. He made an equal effort at being pleasant during our conversation, but I could easily detect a note of suspicion in his voice. He did however confirm that the plant still existed in its entirety and was still housed in a separate factory unit near the Duke Box facility. Doing my best to keep the conversation light and airy, I asked if there had been any interest from companies or individuals in viewing or indeed purchasing it. His response was vague and disinterested but he mentioned that there had been an enquiry from an Australian person some years before. It was as if our conversation was mildly annoying to him but he was putting up with it nonetheless.

My interest piqued, I politely asked if I could 'swing by some time to take a look.' He accepted this request grudgingly and asked me to call him the following week to make an appointment. A seed had been planted in my mind and his casual, disinterested response convinced me he had no real interest in the machines and more importantly, had no idea about the rapidly growing popularity of vinyl records worldwide. It was an opportunity, and a big one at that.

Over the next few days, I researched the vinyl pressing process on YouTube and the internet and learned that very few functioning plants existed worldwide. The ones that did exist were usually worn out old machines, noisy, dirty and in need of constant maintenance. Another factor I discovered was that the companies that originally produced these machines were no longer in business and had shut shop many years before. The facts were stark and simple. You couldn't buy a new record making plant with all the money in the world. My enthusiasm was growing by the day as my research progressed. I was certain that I would find an interested party who would buy the plant, lock stock and barrel. The first thing I had to do was see it, ascertain its condition, photograph it, and then take it from there. Simple. But there was an obstacle in my way. A certain Mr Slade Eatwell.

I managed to make an appointment to meet him at the Duke Box factory the following week. It took me over an hour to get there as I chose a bad route that was severely pot holed, congested, and swarming with police. At the time in Zimbabwe, the police were a scourge on the roads. There were arbitrary road blocks everywhere, and they would fine you for pretty much anything they could find wrong with your vehicle. The officers were set targets by their superiors which had to be met, so they were particularly aggressive in their ticketing. Needless to say a lot of the ticket books were fake as well. I arrived at the Duke Box offices and noticed the flashy Toyota Land Cruiser parked under the car ports. I immediately assumed it belonged to Slade Eatwell. The reception area of the company was impressive and well-decorated but there was an eerie silence about the place. It was as if not a lot of business was actually going on. I introduced myself to the receptionist and told her I had an appointment with Mr Eatwell. She politely asked me to take a seat while she went to inform him I had arrived. Eventually I was led down a corridor and into the office where he sat. "How's it Slade, how are you doing?" I asked cheerfully. He greeted me with fake enthusiasm and motioned for me to sit down before I could shake his hand. To me, this was breaking the golden rule of business. I make a point of shaking hands hands with *anyone* I meet in business. This was a huge red flag.

I proceeded to make pleasant small talk about the dire state of the economy, the roads I had navigated to get there, and his house at Chirundu on the Zambezi River. I could tell the man was doing his best to appear light and cheerful as well, but there was an underlying menace to him. He was a big man, dark and heavy set, slightly overweight and quite morose. When we finally got around to talking about the record plant he told me it was sitting, completely untouched, and had been that way since production stopped in the mid 1990s. I didn't go into too much detail about what they were doing with the plant at the time they ceased production. I decided I would find that out for myself in due course.

So it was after a good twenty minutes of this chit chat, and without being offered tea, that I was invited to ride with him in his Land Cruiser to go and view the record making plant. The journey was less than a few hundred metres. A security guard opened a large set of metal clad gates and we drove into the facility. It was made up of two large factory units. One was being rented by a company that was dealing in small grains and soya beans. There were a few trucks parked, and bored looking workers sitting around. The other was sealed and by the look of the dusty, opaque windows, had been for many years.

We made our way past an outside storage area with wrought iron bars as walls and an asbestos roof. On the inside were a number of scrapped record presses in various states of disrepair, some of their parts having been removed to replace others that had failed. Some were lying on their sides half buried in the red soil, grass, and dirt. All were covered in dust and muck. The lock on the wrought iron gates had long since rusted. I had no reason to take any photographs of this heap of 'scrap,' although I was later to find out it was very valuable indeed. I was shown the massive cooling towers for the plant that were outside the factory on tall solid concrete stands. The huge electric motors, boiler pumps and pipe work baking and rusting in the African sun. I was then led to a large double metal door with peeling grey paint. Again the locks were rusted, but with a bit of effort by the guard, Mr Eatwell and I were able to enter the factory. Nothing could have prepared me for what lay within those doors. The sight that awaited me as I walked in was unbelievable. It was a veritable Aladdin's Cave.

The stale air and dirt dulled windows revealed a shrine to the golden age of vinyl records. A sleeping behemoth. Dormant, but far from dead. There were four record presses bolted into their concrete footings. One still had a blob of vinyl lying near it. Some of them still had the mother stamper plates and labels for 45 RPM records in the press. The record trimming machines were placed nearby, exactly where they had been used all those years ago. Huge steam pipes surrounded the presses with control panels mounted nearby. On the walls were antiquated pressure gauges and heavy electrical wiring. Across the room were the galvanic baths which were surrounded by raised wooden flooring. The control panels, piping, switches and gauges - again, all in place. To the left was a huge work bench with chemicals in glass and plastic bottles and yet more machinery. Huge wooden storage cupboards housed every single stamper the plant had produced, all housed in cardboard sleeves. There were thousands of them. The entire plant was made by Toolex Alpha of Sweden.

Up a set of heavy metal industrial stairs was a large space with shelving, and boxes and boxes of thousands of spares. There were huge bins filled with white label test pressings of singles and albums. Again, too many to count. The entire space the machines, the walls, the floors were all covered by a thick and undisturbed layer of dust. It was like stepping back in time. Like stepping into an abandoned museum. I was then led into a separate room that housed the Neumann Cutting Lathe. Poor quality album sleeves adorned the walls but the lathe and tower were there in perfect condition along with some threadbare seats. This room, being separate from the rest of the factory was dust free and obviously soundproofed.

After the tour, the factory was once again locked, and Eatwell and I made out way back to the Duke Box factory. Once again, we sat down in his office. It was time to get down to brass tacks.

"How much do you want for it?" I asked.

Eatwell shrugged his shoulders and spread his hands in an open gesture.

"Seventy, eighty grand?" he replied hopefully. I nodded in acknowledgement and stood up.

"I'll see what I can do." I thanked him for his time. This time *I* walked towards him to offer my hand. He took it, and thankfully shook it. I took a different route home that was quicker and less congested. But it made no difference to me. My mind was spinning with possibilities. From what I had seen, the plant was in good condition. It could easily be resurrected from the dead. I had no doubt it was worth a fortune. Certainly a lot more than Eatwell had indicated he was expecting. Cash registers were ringing in my brain. Surely there was some adventurous millionaire or rock star out there that would fly to Zimbabwe, and pay me $500,000 or $1,000,000 for it? It was a sure fire winner. I had mentally stored everything Eatwell had told me, and I had the photographs to back it up. It was possibly the biggest opportunity of my life. I could personally contribute to the revival of vinyl, and make a pretty penny in the process. There was only one thing I needed to do. Sell the fucking thing.

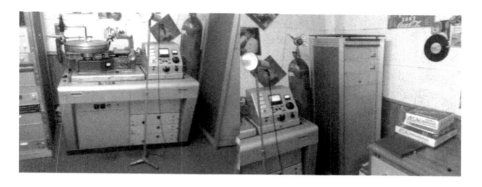

CHAPTER FOUR: THE LISTING

I spent the next few days pondering my next move. What was the best method to do this? How could I raise awareness worldwide? There was a simple solution. eBay. I decided on a simple but very audacious plan. I would list the plant on my eBay account with a price of £160,000. Collection only. I was certain Eatwell was not too tech savvy and would have no clue that I had listed it. The listing would be seen by the world, and the word would no doubt spread to interested parties before long. The listing I made was simple and to the point.

'Entire Vinyl Record Pressing Plant. Toolex Alpha. The location: Harare, Zimbabwe.'

If I recall correctly, the categories it was listed under were 'vinyl records' and 'industrial machinery' Due to it being listed in two categories, it cost maybe £2.50 to do. I made the listing as short and to the point as possible, describing the condition as I saw it. I included my Skype address and phone number for anyone who would want to speak to me about it. I uploaded twelve pictures, the maximum eBay would allow, and made it clear in the listing that the plant would have to be collected in Harare. I did however state that I would assist in the packing and shipping of the plant to the buyer and help with arranging accommodation and transport while they were here. It was a cheeky and bold state-ment to the world and I certainly felt a buzz of excitement as I clicked the button that said 'List your item now.'

I was not on Twitter at the time, and I had no idea that the news had literally spread like wildfire. The view count on my listing rose instantly and dramatically, as did the enquiries and messages that pinged into my inbox. Although my listing clearly stated 'no chancers,' sadly I got a whole lot of these. People from all over the world suddenly wanted to call me on Skype and on my mobile phone. There were people from Italy, Greece, Iceland, the USA, South Africa, New Zealand, Australia. Some were already involved in pressing vinyl and were pretty savvy with their questions. Others were desperately forlorn dreamers with zero capital who just wanted to ask me about the plant and tell me of their desires and longings of starting up a new vinyl pressing factory in some far flung corner of the world. One thing became apparent. The cutting lathe was a focus of many.

Although I had categorically stated in the listing that I would not break up the plant and sell it in separate pieces, I had over ten calls from people literally begging me to sell them the lathe alone. Late one evening I got a Skype video call from two young American girls. We spoke for over an hour. I could tell from the way they spoke and dressed that they were hippy type 'do-gooders' from extremely wealthy families. Their plan was to keep the plant in Zimbabwe and create employment for locals. I had no objections to that. Frankly, I didn't give a fuck what they did with it. I just wanted to sell it and make some money. I think I heard from them once more before they went quiet. The calls and messages streamed in over the next few days, until I got an intriguing call from a man in Ireland by the name of Aiden Foley. Originally from Zimbabwe himself, he was involved in vinyl record pressing in Dublin. Thinking back now, I realise that his was an exploratory phone call. A fishing expedition of sorts. He was trying to find out who I was and what I was up to. He told me he knew

Slade Eatwell and obviously knew of the existence of the machines. He said that he had in fact bought some equipment from Eatwell in the past. I also have no doubt that it was he who alerted Mr Eatwell to my eBay listing. I also have no doubt that he will alert him to the existence of this book. Not that I give a fuck.

The phone call from Eatwell came the next morning.

"Good morning Gordon," he said, sham pleasantry laced with contempt. "I hear you put the plant on eBay for £160,000?"

I was not expecting this.

"Uh, ya, I did Slade," I replied. There was a long pause.

"And what is the plan?" he asked.

"Well Slade, you told me you wanted $80,000, so I have put on a mark up and I am selling it for you. Simple as that." I said.

There was another long pause.

"No, no, no. No ways. You can't put on a mark up like that! Jesus. I tell you what I'll do for you. If you sell it I'll give you 10%. How's that?"

I had to think on my feet. I had been rumbled. The entire plan was in jeopardy. I could have protested this sudden change of tune, but I needed to at least make something of it. I was left with little choice in the matter.

"Ok," I said. "I'll leave the listing up and we will see what comes of it."

He agreed sullenly, and the conversation was over. I felt deflated and was surprised as to how he got to know of it in the first place. However, I kept the eBay listing live and fielded the various calls and messages that came through. It was perhaps two days later that I received another call from Eatwell. He informed me that he had *suddenly* received *numerous* calls from people around the world who were interested in buying the plant and that *he* would take it from there. In other words, my services were no longer required. My efforts had come to zero. It was with a heavy heart, but knowing that at least I had tried, that I clicked the 'End my listing now' button on eBay. At the time I thought the mission was over. The plan had fallen through. But nothing could have been further from the truth. In fact, the journey had only just begun.

CHAPTER FIVE: SIX MONTHS LATER

During the months that followed, and despite my listing being taken down, I received countless telephone and Skype calls from people around the world. Much to their disappointment, I informed them all that the plant was no longer for sale. I too was sad that it hadn't worked out, but I had moved on with my various businesses and was keeping myself busy enough. Then one morning, completely out of the blue, I received a call from Slade Eatwell. He sounded rather sad and down and asked if I would visit him later in the week at the Duke Box offices. He told me that the people who had shown interest in the plant had let him down, and wanted to discuss it with me again. I was genuinely surprised and agreed to meet him later that week. During the following days I racked my brain as to what might have gone wrong. Why would such a valuable set of machinery still be unsold?

On the day of the appointment, I took the long drive to the dusty, potholed industrial site of Southerton. I was feeling optimistic and hopeful that I would once again be granted permission to sell the plant. I knew from the many, many calls I had received that, given the chance, there would be a good chance I would succeed. After my arrival was announced, I was led through to the office of a very different Mr Slade Eatwell. Instead of the sullen and suspicious man I had previously dealt with, I found him to be almost genuinely friendly. He even shook my hand as he offered me a seat.

What followed was an hour long conversation in which I found out that there indeed had been interested parties from Australia and South Africa, but none of these had even bothered to make the trip to Zimbabwe to see the plant. Like the many others who had contacted me, they were all chancers. He also told me that there had been some political interference from a certain government minister, Professor Jonathan Moyo, who at the time was the Minister of Higher Education in the Zimbabwe government. A despised character in Zimbabwe, he had previously been the Minister of Information and was responsible for the AIPPA and POSA restrictive legislation which had shut down radio stations, barred media organisations and generally caused a lot of suffering to anyone who was against the Mugabe Government. He was also the owner of a recording studio in Harare, and many say responsible for the downfall of various musicians who he roped into producing political songs - one of them being the late Andy Brown, who I have mentioned earlier in this story. Moyo was also linked to cases of corruption in Kenya and Zimbabwe.

Currently in exile having fled after the fall of Mugabe, his whereabouts are unknown. At the time, Eatwell told me he had shown interest in the plant, but he had not heard from him in months. He then went on to question me about the mechanics of actually selling and shipping the plant from Zimbabwe to its final destination. He was worried if there would be questions asked or if there would be any risk of trouble. I explained, for example, that if I chose to sell my brick making machine to a buyer in South Africa, there was no way anyone could possibly stop me from doing so as it was my machine and I could sell it to whom I want regardless of where they were. He saw my explanation as reasonable and nodded in agreement. I was starting to become aware that Eatwell was a rather naïve and unsophisticated individual. It was starting to look like I was once again going to be tasked with selling Africa's lost vinyl pressing plant. Our conversation continued with pressing questions for another hour, and not once was I offered a cup of tea. Eatwell explained that he was leaving on a family holiday to the UK in a few days and would be away for six weeks.

After what seemed an age I put it straight to him.

"So, Slade, would you like me to try and sell it again?"

"Yup, I think so," he replied. I stood up, shook his hand, and left the Duke Box facility. As I took the long drive home, my mind was once again buzzing with possibilities. My enthusiasm was fired once again. The job was on, even if it was only for ten percent.

CHAPTER SIX: THE RE-LISTING

It was that very night that I trawled through my unsold items on eBay until I found my original listing for the record plant. I casually clicked on the Sell Similar button and added that the item was being re-listed due to a let down and was now available again for sale. It was only many months afterwards that I realised the impact the listing had had on the media and the internet. Unknowingly, I had set it on fire. There were countless articles on international news sites, Facebook and Twitter. All of these seemed to be slightly amused at the sheer audacity of the listing itself and more so the asking price. Looking back on the comments, I remember some people were incredulous, while others were more complimentary, pointing out that actually, given the staggering rise in the popularity of vinyl, anyone with a sound business brain should realise very quickly that the price wasn't actually that outrageous at all. And so, once again began the barrage of calls and messages from around the world. And the requests to purchase the Neumann Cutting Lathe on its own. This despite the fact that the listing clearly stated I would not break up the plant under any circumstances.

The calls and Skype requests came in day and night. From the USA, Canada, Italy, France, Germany, Australia and New Zealand. Of particular amusement to me was one seemingly unscrupulous lady from South Africa who repeatedly called saying what an important investment it was, and that she had extremely powerful backers with unlimited finance. She wanted to conclude the deal there and then on the phone. She suggested she would 'remove the plant and pay later.' I laughed that one off pretty quickly. My message to everyone was clear and simple.

"Get on a plane. Fly to Harare. I will pick you up and show you the plant. I will even suggest some decent accommodation for you."

I had to continuously go through the motions of answering these various questions and repeating this message until finally I received a particularly interesting call one Saturday around lunch time. I knew from the country code that the person was calling from the UK. The man was well-spoken and I could tell from the start that although his was a kindly, good-natured voice, there was no doubt he knew exactly what he was talking about. I could also tell from his voice that he was a slightly older man. Politely, he introduced himself as Roy Matthews, a previous employee of EMI, UK. I told him it was a huge relief to be finally talking to someone who actually knew what they were on about and not some chancer or dreamer from God-knows-where. We had a bit of a laugh about this and our conversation continued. He explained that although he was retired, he had been retained by a Polish company to procure a vinyl record pressing plant, and he had come across my listing on the internet.

Without going into too much detail he explained that the company in Poland was of considerable size and was currently involved in the production of CDs and DVDs. We spoke for a good amount of time and seemed to develop a good rapport. In the end, I explained that there was really only one way to go about it. Get on a plane. Fly to Harare. I will pick you up and show you the plant. After a good long talk, he concluded by thanking me for my time and telling me that he would more than likely call me back the following Monday. I knew from the start that this had been an important call and would likely lead to a visit, if not a sale.

After we hung up I stored his number in my phone simply as 'Roy Machines' I had absolutely no idea of the astonishing importance and significance of this man in the very development and history of vinyl records as we know them. Roy Matthews, apart from being a really great bloke, is an absolute legend. Google him.

CHAPTER SEVEN: THE PLANNING

As promised, what followed the next week were a series of phone calls from Roy, sometimes up to three calls a day. All of them were pleasant and cordial, but very much to the point. Without mentioning a name he always referred to his boss in Poland as his 'principal' although he did mention once that the company was called Takt. I did Google the name one night and although the website was a bit hard to navigate, I could clearly see it was a substantial concern. He also mentioned that he had once travelled to South Africa in the 1980s to help set up a cassette factory in Johannesburg. He did say that one of their concerns, should they visit, was that of personal safety. The only global media that was being portrayed at the time about Zimbabwe was extremely negative - political violence, chaos and oppression under the Mugabe regime. In a nutshell, there was no good news, despite Zimbabwe being one of the most beautiful countries in Africa. I assured him that Zimbabwe was, and remains, far safer than South Africa in terms of violent crime. Zimbabweans are a gentle, peaceful people, whereas in South Africa one has to be very aware of potential danger at all times. And so the many calls and emails continued for days between us, until it was finally confirmed that Roy and his 'principal' would fly out to Harare the following week. The trip would be for three nights only, with the second day solely dedicated to viewing and inspecting the record plant. Next came the issue of accommodation. Roy had told me that wifi was essential, and I wanted them to have the very best possible experience. I advised them to book into the luxury Amanzi Lodge in Greystone Park - a leafy area in the Northern Suburbs of Harare. Roy emailed me and told me that he would be travelling with Mr Andrzej Mackiewicz, the managing director of Takt, Poland. He also told me that despite having being hired by them, they had never met in person, and would only do so at Heathrow airport, in London. They were flying business class and due to arrive the following Tuesday afternoon at 1.45pm on the Ethiopian Airways flight from Addis Ababa. I would meet them at the arrivals hall at Harare airport and take them to their Lodge. I could hardly believe it. My plan was coming together. It was actually happening. Slade Eatwell was far away in the UK, unable to meddle and I had arranged full unimpeded access to the factory that housed the plant in his absence. It was all systems go.

CHAPTER EIGHT: THE ARRIVAL

I spent the weekend fretting. I had no idea who these people were or what to expect. I worried about how I should dress to meet them. It was September in Zimbabwe and the weather is very hot in that month, as we approach the rainy season which is our summer. I worried about what vehicle to use. At the time I only had a pickup truck and a small run around type car. Neither were suitable for this purpose. Eventually, my girlfriend at the time suggested that I simply be myself and dress as usual for the time of year. Long shorts, t-shirt, and sandals. She also suggested that I use her vehicle which was a smart, relatively new 4x4 with air conditioning. I agreed and so it was decided.

On the Monday I printed out a sheet of paper with the names 'Mr Roy Matthews' and 'Mr Andrzej Mackiewicz' on it, so they would recognise me as they walked out of the arrivals hall. I was feeling a mixture of excitement and trepidation. There was no way to predict what the outcome of this would be. There was a last minute phone call from Roy to let me know he was on his way to the station to catch his train to Heathrow. He sounded his usual relaxed and pleasant self. That night I lay awake for hours wondering what to expect. Everything was in place. The accommodation I had arranged at Amanzi Lodge was opulent. The receptionist from Duke Box and a former worker from the record pressing plant would meet us at the facility at 8.30am on the Wednesday. What could possibly go wrong?

I left my house early on the Tuesday to make sure I was at the airport as the plane arrived. There is a restaurant upstairs with a full view of the arrivals hall, and I watched as the passengers from the Ethiopian Airways flight queued at immigration. Immediately I picked out two men. One older and taller, the other shorter in stature, busying himself with the immigration forms. Both were smartly dressed. I had no doubt they were Roy and Andrzej. As they cleared immigration I raced downstairs to greet them as they came through the arrivals area. They saw my sign as soon they walked through and I walked forward to introduce myself. I first shook hands with Roy. He was exactly as I had expected. Tall, well-dressed, warm and friendly. Next was Andrzej, again, a very amiable chap with a ready smile and a keen eye. He introduced himself in excellent English and with a firm handshake. I could tell this man meant business.

As we walked out of the airport building I asked about the flight. They both replied saying Ethiopian business class had been excellent. They paused briefly as we walked into the warm afternoon sun. "Welcome to Zimbabwe," I said, seeing the pleasure in their faces.

"First time in Africa!" said Andrzej with a grin. I liked both of them immediately. The whole thing was getting off to a great start. We loaded their bags into the back of the vehicle in the sun and I was glad I had decided to use my girlfriend's car. The heat was fierce and the air conditioning was welcome. Andrzej, being a gentleman, offered the front passenger seat to Roy as he was so tall. We made our way out of the airport area and towards the city. As we drove Roy casually asked the question I knew would come.

"So, Gordon, how did you come by this plant?"

I replied, saying that I was in a partnership in it and had been for some time. I explained that the other partner was away on holiday in the UK and was due to return soon, and that I would handle everything during their visit. This explanation seemed satisfactory to both of them and we chatted happily as we made our way towards the affluent Northern suburbs of Harare. Both of them seemed amazed by the greenery and order on the roads in Harare. They explained that they had half expected a dusty shanty town. Their preconceptions had clearly been affected by the negative press Zimbabwe had been getting. We were all in good spirits as we arrived at the ornate gates of Amanzi Lodge and I could tell Roy and Andrzej were both very impressed by the lush tropical gardens. I dropped them at the reception and told them both I would leave them to settle into their rooms and then collect them for dinner at 6.30pm sharp. As I drove out of the gates to go home I had a good feeling about both of my guests. Both Roy and Andrzej were pleasant and congenial, and although their mission was purely business, I knew that we would all enjoy their trip. I dressed smart for dinner as I had booked us into Amanzi Restaurant, part of the group that owned the lodge. In keeping with the lodge, the restaurant is stylish and upmarket, again set in lush manicured gardens.

I arrived in the cool of the evening at the lodge to find them refreshed and waiting for me in the reception area.

"I have to find a reason to come back to this amazing place!" Andrzej exclaimed as I walked in.

"I know, it's very nice isn't it?" I said. "Wait until we get to the restaurant."

The drive took ten minutes, we parked and were ushered to our outdoor table by our waiter. Roy and I ordered a beer each while Andrzej ordered a sparkling water. It was when our drinks arrived that I noticed that Roy's right hand had a slight tremor and he was battling to pour his beer.

"Can I assist you with that Roy?" I asked casually.

"Thank you Gordon, yes please," he said. I poured the beer and we went on to order our food. Roy and Andrzej both ordered the fillet steak. This came highly recommended by me. Zimbabwean beef is well-known for its superb flavour. What followed was a superb evening talking mainly about vinyl records. I set the scene for both of them, describing the factory and plant like a museum. A monument to a bygone age. I described the machinery in minute detail; the dust and grime on the windows and the blob of vinyl that had been left near the one record press. Although my guests were clearly tired from the travelling there was no mistaking the glint of excitement in their eyes. After the meal I dropped them both at the lodge and told them I would be back to collect them at 8am the following day. All of us were enlivened. It was finally happening. Africa's lost vinyl plant was about to be seen by some serious potential buyers.

CHAPTER NINE: THE FACTORY VISIT

I arrived at the lodge as promised at 8am to find Roy and Andrzej both refreshed and waiting eagerly. We took the drive straight through the city centre down Samora Machel Avenue and left into Rotten Row. I knew it would be the quickest way to get to the factory. We would avoid the potholed route through Mbare, and my guests would get to see what the actual city centre looked like. I played the tour guide as I showed them the Reserve Bank and other buildings of interest. Again, they were surprised by the level of sophistication of the city and the glass covered skyscrapers. They were also aware of the beggars and street kids that came to the windows at every traffic light. Eventually we made it through the traffic to Southerton and to the gates of the factory.

As I had arranged, the receptionist from Duke Box was waiting for us along with an ex-worker from the record plant, Albert. The tension was palpable as we locked the vehicle and took the short dusty walk over to the steel doors of the facility. Like before, the locks took a bit of persuading but eventually the five of us walked into the stale air and dimmed light of the factory floor.

"Wow!" said Andrzej, as he stopped to gaze in awe around him. "It's exactly like you said, Gordon. Just like a museum."

Roy, on the other hand, was all about business, and proceeded to inspect the presses individually. At the time, there was very little industrial activity in Southerton, and the place had an eerie silence about it. The very machines responsible for reproducing music, their hissing and clanking steam-powered bulk sat in hushed tranquility. Albert, a cheerful and elderly ex-employee competed with me in my role as tour guide. Enthusiastically, he pointed out each machine and explained what it did. Although both Roy and Andrzej were fully aware of their function, they went along with it and I could see they were thoroughly enjoying the 'tour'. Andrzej took numerous pictures of everything as we made our way meticulously through the various machinery. After taking a detailed look at the presses and the galvanic baths we were led into the nerve centre of the plant - the cutting room.

The soundproof door was unlocked, the light turned on and we were finally able to view the Neumann Cutting Lathe in all its glory. Soon enough, the receptionist made her excuses and left the four of us to continue our inspection. Both Roy and Andrzej were armed with clipboards and cameras and there was not one section of the plant that wasn't documented and logged down in minute detail. This was a hot, dirty, and time-consuming task, but not one of us lost enthusiasm or interest. Albert led us upstairs to the industrial shelves that held literally thousand of spares, including many for the cutting lathe. The motors for these lathes are very heavy, rounded, black square blocks with the shafts protruding from the top. There were at least two brand new, unused

examples of these. Nothing escaped the scrutiny of Roy and Andrzej, including the cooling towers and pumps which were situated outside the factory. Roy took a very precarious climb up the
concrete and metal structure in the blazing sun to log the make,
horsepower, and serial numbers of the pump motors. Both Andrzej and myself were seriously concerned for his safety as he did
this and I made a casual joke about him having travel health insurance should he be injured. Of particular interest to them was
the outside storage area that housed the 'scrap.' Although we
failed to open the rusty lock, Roy and Andrzej took their time
noting what was housed behind the corroded iron work that held
the asbestos roof.

Although I found him to be very affable, I could sense a certain
intensity about Andrzej. He was a driven man, constantly on his
phone talking in Polish to his colleagues in Krakow.

There was no doubt this man was all about business. It was four
hours later when a very sweaty Andrzej declared that he and Roy
were satisfied. They had seen enough. Cordial and polite to the
end, they never once discussed their thoughts or what they were
logging on their clipboards. It was after a thorough washing of
hands and arms that we thanked Albert for his efforts and grate-
fully entered the air conditioning of the car. There was a distinct
feeling of satisfaction and accomplishment as we took the Simon
Mazorodze Road out of Southerton and back towards the city
centre. I decided to show my guests some sights on the way back,
so I took a route through the Avenues past the Harare Sports
Club with its immaculate cricket ground. We drove past the

Royal Harare Golf Club and State House as we made our way to the plush and modern Borrowdale Village for a spot of lunch.

"You can tell why the English wanted this place." said Roy thoughtfully as he admired the colonial architecture. "It's beautiful."

The opulence of the shopping centre that is a hub of the wealthy of Harare was a far cry from the potholed and dystopian industrial site of Southerton. We made our way in the heat through the palm trees of the car park and into the restaurant adjacent to the Spar Supermarket. Again the air conditioning was a relief. Andrzej ordered a large salad, while Roy and I opted for the fish and chips. It was clear they were surprised by what they were seeing. Here there were no beggars or street kids. No dusty potholed roads with abandoned factories baking in the sun. Here was a huge modern, cosmopolitan shopping centre with green verges and irrigation. Here, the wealthy of all races parked their flashy 4x4s and Mercedes vehicles while they shopped and dined in luxury. It was a big contrast. We spoke nothing of the record plant as we ate, but Andrzej did take my phone number when Roy excused himself to go to the toilet. When he returned, we agreed that I would take them to my favourite restaurant that evening. I explained that although it was certainly not as fancy as Amanzi, the food was superb. After the meal I asked Roy and Andrzej what their plans were that afternoon. They had none. I suggested that I take them on a short tour where they could get a taste of the real Africa. Again this was agreed and we left Borrowdale Village after Roy and Andrzej both bought themselves a copy of the gorgeous coffee table book, 'Beneath a Zimbabwe Sun' by

Beverley Whyte. I dropped them at their lodge to give them a chance to rest and freshen up, and told them I would return in an hour to collect them. I purposely neglected to tell them the destination of our tour, preferring to leave that a surprise. We would be going to a mountain range with absolutely spectacular views, not far out of Harare. A place that few tourists ever get to see, and with the right vehicle, and some serious nerves, one could drive all the way up to the summit.

CHAPTER TEN: NGOMOKURIRA
MOUNTAIN

I returned as promised and we made our way to Enterprise Road. Turning left we drove through the affluent suburb of Glen Lorne, sometimes called Corruption Hills due to the massive gaudy mansions built by the politically connected. Roy and Andrzej marvelled at the startling gap between the rich and poor as we drove. After passing the Umwinsidale turn-off we arrived at the Shamva/Mutoko fork. We took a right and finally drove out of the city and into the countryside. As we drove, I fielded many questions about farming and productivity on the ground since Mugabe's chaotic land reform programme. Our discussions were open and honest, and I did my best to give them a clear picture of what was actually going on in the country. Fifteen minutes later we took a left turn at a rural bottle store and took the dirt road that leads to Ngomokurira Mountain. The road had been severely damaged by rains, and was in a rough state but we made our way carefully through the fields and hillocks, past the mud huts and villages. Although it was very hot and dusty we were comfortably cocooned in our air conditioned vehicle. Tall yellow grass grew from the rich red soil between the grey granite rocky outcrops and above us was a clear blue sky. My guests were thoroughly enjoying the rural surroundings and we stopped frequently to allow them to snap pictures of villages and scenic views.

It was twenty minutes later when we finally arrived at the turn off to the 'road' that leads to the summit. Had we carried on for another ten minutes we would have driven around to the front of the mountain and I'm certain that had Roy and Andrzej seen it from there, they would have flatly refused to attempt the drive to the top. Ngomokurira Mountain is a massive granite behemoth when viewed from the front. When I say 'road,' I say it lightly. It is more of a broken, rocky trail that slowly winds its way upwards through the Msasa forests and boulders until one comes to the actual rock of the huge mountain. At the turn off we were surrounded by a group of kids all vying for the opportunity to guide us to the summit. The trail upwards is complicated and impassable in areas so a guide is imperative if one is to actually get to the top. I chose a guide who jumped in the back with Andrzej, and we began the slow arduous journey up the mountain with Roy and Andrzej both gripping the interior door handles to avoid being thrown around as we went.

Eventually, and after a few failed attempts, we made it to the clearing at the base at the rear of the giant rock that is Ngomokurira Mountain. Already the views were spectacular from there and my guests were suitably impressed. They had no idea that we still had to navigate the steep rock trail that led to the summit. It was when we turned left and slowly started climbing the seemingly forty five degree rock slope that I heard the words, "oh my God" from Andrzej in the back. In actual fact, this last section of the mountain is much easier than the first, as the rock is not broken and has more than enough grip for the tyres. It is simply the angle of ascent that is alarming to the uninitiated.

Eventually, and to the great relief of Andrzej, we made it to the upper levels and started towards the beacon at the summit. I can only describe the reaction of my guests to the view as one of being absolutely flabbergasted. To say they were thrilled would be an understatement. Amid exclamations of astonishment from my guests, we parked and slowly made our way towards the beacon at the summit. It was when Andrzej and I had reached the beacon that we turned around to see Roy taking a fall on the rocks. He was wearing standard leather work shoes which were hardly suitable for climbing.

"Roy!" shouted Andrzej in panic, as he raced down the slope to assist our colleague.

Thankfully Roy managed to stabilise himself and was not injured at all. He promptly got to his feet and proceeded up to the beacon where I stood.

"I cannot believe we are here!" said Andrzej, as he stared out at the 360 degree view in amazement.

We sat up there quietly for fifteen minutes taking in our surroundings. I mentioned to Andrzej that there was a recently-discovered cave with bushman paintings not far down the slope to the front of the mountain. This pricked his interest and although

I warned him the climb was steep and tough, he insisted he would like to see it. As he walked off through the forest at the top of the mountain with the guide, I spoke to Roy.

"Do you think he's interested Roy?" I asked. Ever the professional and not giving too much away he replied.

"I think there might be something we can do."

I left it at that. Roy and I sat in the afternoon sun in comfortable silence as we awaited the return of Andrzej from the cave. It was perhaps twenty minutes later when Roy and I saw Andrzej and the guide making their way back up the mountain towards us. Andrzej was red in the face, sweating profusely and desperately in need of some of the bottled water I had brought for us. The climb had been harder than he expected and he was angry at himself for being so unfit. To me this was another example of how hard Andrzej drove himself both personally and in business. After he had recovered, we took a slow drive down the mountain in the fading light of the afternoon. At the base of the mountain we tipped our guide and made our way back up the dirt road. Not far from the mountain is a rural bottle store which I knew stocked ice cold drinks. I stopped and asked my guests if they would like a cold beer. Roy was in full agreement to this idea. Andrzej ordered a soft drink.

We made our way happily back to the main road and to Amanzi Lodge. By the time we arrived the sun had set and the evening was cool. I dropped them at the reception and told them I would be back in an hour to collect them for dinner. Feeling exhausted, I came home for a quick shower and a change of clothes. I returned on time to find Roy and Andrzej waiting as usual in the reception area. We took the slow drive in the dark through the heavy traffic to the Avenues area of Harare. Our destination, The Coimbra Restaurant - home of the finest peri-peri chicken in the world.

CHAPTER ELEVEN: THE OFFER

The good smells from the restaurant drifted into the car park as we disembarked. We were led to my usual table by a waiter called Chengerai. I have known him for years and he is so popular, he even has his own business card. Roy and I opted for beer while Andrzej ordered the usual mineral water. As is tradition at The Coimbra, we were given a bowl of sliced bread rolls along with two small jugs of sauces. One garlic, the other peri peri chicken dripping. I instructed my guests as to The Coimbra protocol of pouring some of each sauce into a side plate, buttering a piece of bread and dipping it. Roy battled a bit with his right hand shaking, but this was very well-received by both of them. Although we were all enjoying ourselves, there was a certain tension about the guests. I had booked them on a trip to Chengeta Safari Lodge the following day and they were due to fly out the next morning. This would be the last time I would see them. I had a feeling there would be some sort of discussion that night. As usual, the chicken and chips were delectable. It was after our plates were cleared and we had ordered another drink that they chose their moment.

"Can we talk openly here Gordon?" asked Andrzej.

"Sure, of course we can." I replied, reassuring him. It was then that Roy took over.

"Gordon, it was fascinating to see the machines today, and I have to say that they are in remarkable condition."

"Oh, ok," I replied cheerfully.

"The difficult thing is putting a value on them. As you know it's impossible to actually buy these machines at the moment."

I nodded in understanding. He went on.

"Anyway, you are asking £160,000 but we have come up with an offer which we think is reasonable. We would like to offer you $120,000."

This was it. An offer on the table. I had to think on my feet. Although I was certain that Slade Eatwell would accept the figure, I couldn't give them a straight answer there and then. He was in the UK on holiday and I would need to call him the following day. I nodded calmly as a million thoughts raced through my mind. As I prepared to speak, Andrzej interjected suddenly.

"Gordon, we can do $124 000. That is our budget."

Again I paused.

"Well that sounds like a good offer, and I'm sure Slade will agree . I'll have to call him tomorrow morning to be certain, but as I said, I think that will be fine."

"We were hoping to open the champagne tonight," said Andrzej hopefully.

Again I explained my situation emphasising that, although I was certain it would be agreed, I could not say yes without the go ahead from Eatwell. I promised that I would call them the following morning with the answer. Although there was a hint of disappointment in Andrzej, he seemed to understand my predicament, and the evening continued as well as it had started. I dropped them both at the lodge knowing I would not see them again on that trip, and assured them that I would have a firm answer by 12pm the following day. My head was buzzing as I took the drive home. I lay awake that night wondering what Eatwell would say. In the end I decided that he would more than likely accept it. After all it was a good $40,000 more than he had initially said he wanted and he hadn't lifted a finger. I awoke the next day and began trying to call Slade Eatwell on the UK number I had been given by the receptionist at Duke Box. The number was a landline, but to my great frustration there was no reply. It was 11.45am when finally the phone was answered by an English-sounding lady. I introduced myself and asked to speak to Slade. I was then put on hold for a good five minutes as I watched the clock slowly move towards 12pm.

Eventually a very hungover Eatwell picked up the phone and said, "Hello?"

Forgoing any pleasantries, I got straight to business. "Slade, this is Gordon. I've had a firm offer on the record plant of $124,000. These guys are serious. What do you think?"

There was a short pause, followed by his reply. "Ya…that sounds fine."

"Are you sure Slade?" I asked.

"Ya, that's fine Gordon. Let's do it."

I looked at the clock as I thanked him and hung up.

There was five minutes to go before 12pm, when I had said I would call Andrzej and Roy. I was sure their nerves would be as frayed as mine by that late stage. I finally got through to Andrzej as they were on a game drive at the safari lodge. Although his voice was hushed as they were tracking animals at the time, I could tell he was overjoyed at the news. He promised to call me later that evening when they returned from the safari. As I hung up, I was left feeling a mixture of emotions. Of course, I was thrilled that I had put it all together, but there was a distinct feeling of trepidation that went along with it. A deep-seated worry that a certain individual could scupper the entire deal. And could do so simply on a whim. The individual in question was Mr Slade Eatwell. And in time, it turned out my fears were not unfounded.

CHAPTER TWELVE: THE FINER DETAILS

Roy and Andrzej returned late from Chengeta Safari Lodge that night. The phone call only came the following morning. Both of them had thoroughly enjoyed their day of game viewing and canoeing in the bush. They thanked me for my efforts and told me they would be in contact once they got back to their respective homes and offices. The Ethiopian Airways flight was due to leave at 3.15pm, and they had arranged a taxi from the lodge to the airport. Having heard nothing more from Eatwell, I never mentioned him to them, deciding to let sleeping dogs lie. After all, it was agreed. The deal was on. It was two days later that I started receiving calls and emails from Andrzej. The eBay listing was still live and I had decided to leave it that way until I was paid. Obviously Roy and Andrzej wanted it removed so my bank details were requested as a matter of urgency. Sure enough, and as promised, the following day the funds appeared in my account. I clicked the 'End my listing' button and it was gone.

What followed was a never-ending train of emails and messages from Andrzej. It was clear that he wanted to move, and move quickly. I was instructed to find a rigging company with forklifts, cranes, and heavy transport. Also needed was a reputable international shipping company and an insurance broker. All of this needed to be done within a week, as Andrzej and Roy had booked their return flights in ten days and would want to oversee the removal of the entire plant from the facility in Southerton whilst they were here. It was all happening, and happening fast. I managed to secure the services of a crane hire and rigging company in Harare. We made one site visit to the factory to ascertain the scale of the job. I explained to the owner that it was an international concern who were buying the plant so payment would not be an issue. The company also had forklifts and Hiab fitted long bed trucks. The time frame for such a job was put at two days. Quotations were sent to me and forwarded to Andrzej. Next, I visited the offices of Speedlink Cargo in Msasa. I explained what I needed doing, and established a relationship with the person who would handle the shipment. I assumed it would more than likely require a forty foot container which would travel by road through Zimbabwe and Mozambique to the port of Beira. From there it would travel by ship to the port city of Gdansk, Poland, and then on to Krakow.

Next I called Insurance Services Harare and spoke to the owner, Kevin Elkington. I explained what we were doing and what was needed. He said there would be no problem with insuring the shipment and that he would visit us once we had delivered the machines to the shipping company. It was all coming together. Satisfied that I had covered all the bases, I emailed Andrzej to tell him everything was in place. I had booked them into a lodge in Harare that was run by friends of mine. Although not as smart and stylish as Amanzi it would offer all Roy and Andrzej needed, and was situated nearby in the leafy suburb of Glen Lorne. Added to that, I organised a vehicle and a driver for my guests for the duration of their stay. They were booked to be in Zimbabwe for five nights only and everything would need to be done in that short time frame. It was a tall order with no room for errors, but I thought, with a bit of luck, it would be doable. It was a few days later that I received a call from Slade Eatwell, who had returned from his holiday in the UK.

He had obviously got out of the wrong side of his bed that morning and phoned me for a fat moan.

"Listen Gordon, I'm a bit worried about this whole thing. I don't know who these people are and if I can trust them. I'm worried about exporting the machines and I'm thinking about calling the whole thing off."

Red flags and alarm bells started going off in my brain. The moody, insecure, and unpredictable Eatwell was acting out my greatest fears. After all Roy, Andrzej and myself had done, he was willing to throw it all away at the drop of a hat. It was as if I was dealing with a spoilt child.

"Slade, these guys travelled business class from Poland and the UK respectively. They stayed at Amanzi Lodge. I have arranged the riggers, the forklifts, the insurance and the shipping. They are on their way back here next week to conclude this. These guys are very serious indeed."

My assurances had a calming effect on him, and he grunted his approval. I hung up, feeling shaken. The volatile and unpredictable Eatwell had struck, and I wondered if he would do so again.

CHAPTER THIRTEEN: THE GUESTS RETURN

It was because of that phone call from Eatwell that I spent the weekend with an uneasy feeling in my stomach. Roy and Andrzej were due to arrive the following Monday. Crunch time was approaching fast. I had organised the rigging company to be on site on the Tuesday morning to begin the removal of the machines, but before any work could commence, there would be the crucial meeting with Eatwell at the Duke Box offices. Everything was riding on that. In a state of semi-panic, I contacted a trusted friend for advice.

"Gordon, if your nose is clean, you have nothing to worry about," he said.

This was a small comfort to me. I had been 100% open with everyone, and if Eatwell decided to pull out at such a late stage, it would be on him. He would look like the fool. And so the following Monday, I collected Roy and Andrzej from the airport and drove them to the new lodge in Glen Lorne. Although Roy was his usual calm and pleasant self, I detected a certain tension in Andrzej. As I pressed the buzzer for the electric gate there was a strange garbled sound from the intercom. The electronic bell noise was wobbly and unsteady. I wondered to myself if this was a harbinger of things to come. Eventually we got inside where Roy and Andrzej were both shown their rooms. I sat near the pool while I waited for them. The owner, my friend Colin Hopley, sat with me whilst we waited for them to freshen up and come out.

Roy was first to arrive and he greeted Colin with his usual charm and pleasantry. He sat with us and commented on the beauty of the lodge and the gardens. While they chatted, I watched the window of Andrzej's room nervously. As he tried to close the curtain the railing fell down with a crash. Although this was soon rectified, I had the distinct feeling that this was slowly turning into a comedy of errors.

Eventually Andrzej arrived and met the owner, after which we took a drive to Msasa to pick up some tools they needed to dismantle the Neumann Cutting Lathe. As we browsed the giant hardware shop for allen keys and other equipment, I realised that Andrzej was tired and stressed. It had been a long journey, and there was much that could go wrong. I found myself wishing I had taken a Valium prior to their arrival. Roy had been given precise instructions and diagrams from an old colleague on how to dismantle the lathe and, being such a fragile and rare piece of equipment, it was vital that this be done to the letter. I had made the crucial appointment with Eatwell the following morning at 8.30am sharp. Andrzej asked me to call him to confirm this, but I repeatedly found his mobile phone unreachable. This was both embarrassing and frustrating for me. Although I did my best to portray an image of calm, I was pretty much freaking out on the inside. It was on my last failed attempt back at the lodge that Andrzej asked.

"What is the problem with this guy, Gordon?"

"Let's just say that Slade is a difficult person," I said, shaking my head. "It will all be fine, don't worry."

As my guests were tired, I left them to have dinner at their lodge and went home. Eventually that evening I managed to get through to Eatwell who confirmed the meeting the following day. I called Andrzej to inform him and put his mind at ease. I spent a troubled night worrying about what that next day would bring. We were almost there. Almost.

CHAPTER FOURTEEN: THE APPOINTMENT

I arrived at the lodge to find Roy and Andrzej rested and cheerful. This was a big relief for me after the tension of the previous day. With our driver following in the hired vehicle, we made our way through the city and on to the industrial site of Southerton. We stopped briefly outside the factory that housed the record plant to greet the riggers who were there waiting to start work. I was relieved to see Eatwell's Land Cruiser parked under the awnings at Duke Box. From the reception, we were ushered in to his office. I can only compare Slade Eatwell's demeanour and mannerisms that morning to one of a jovial clown. He greeted us all with warm handshakes and laughter as he offered us seats. A far cry from the brooding suspicious man I knew.

Before we got down to business, there was a bit of banter and small talk regarding the reconditioned jukeboxes and pinball machines on display. Both Roy and Andrzej wanted to buy one. Finally it came down to business.

"So you've come to buy the record machines?" said Eatwell happily.

"That is correct," said Andrzej.

"And the price is $124.000?"

"Correct," said Andrzej.

"Ok, well that sounds fine. And you have your equipment ready dismantle and remove everything?"

"Yup, everyone is ready to start work," I said.

"Ok, well let's do it!" Eatwell said enthusiastically.

We all thanked him, shook hands, and left the Duke Box factory. I, for one, was feeling a huge sense of relief. It had gone well, with no opposition from Eatwell. Apart from the fake nicety and politeness, he seemed genuine and trusting for now. This was good. We took the short drive to the vinyl plant with Albert, the old worker from the factory, and met up with the rigging crew. The brief was simple. Every single bit of equipment or machinery that had anything to do with the vinyl record manufacturing process was to be carefully dismantled and removed. This meant everything from the smallest rubber pipette to the massive pumps and galvanic baths. There were ten workers from the rigging company, and I had brought three of my own to assist. The thirty tonne flat bed truck was reversed into position near the factory doors, the forklift was driven in and so began the gargantuan task of removing Africa's lost vinyl record pressing plant.

The riggers came equipped with the heavy tools needed to unbolt the vinyl presses from their concrete mountings. They set about doing this immediately whilst Roy and Andrzej concentrated on the fiddly and complicated task of dismantling the Neumann Cutting Lathe. It was hot and dirty work, but before long the bolts from the first press were removed, a heavy chain was attached and the forklift carefully raised it from where it had sat for so many years in silence. The incredibly heavy press swung precariously from the forklift as it trundled out of the doors, but eventually it was loaded safely onto the flat bed truck and secured with chains. It was when the second press was being removed that the explosion came. Roy and Andrzej had taken a break from the cutting room to watch it being raised. Albert had neglected to turn off a valve or similar, and as the press was lifted there was an almighty boom, followed by the violent hissing of trapped air. Andrzej had been standing right in front of the press as it happened. He turned to look at me, and although he was uninjured, he was covered from head to toe in dirty old hydraulic oil. Much later, we all laughed heartily at this mishap, but at the time I was quite alarmed at the sight of the smart, high powered Polish businessman standing there dripping with oil and grease.

A huge pool of oil quickly formed on the factory floor effectively turning it into an ice skating rink. This as the October heat became more and more intense. Albert and my workers quickly went about mopping and scooping it up, and before long the floor was cleaned and work could continue. The accident did nothing to stop us, and we continued through the morning methodically disconnecting and removing the giant presses, control boards, pumps, piping and switch gear. By lunch time, although we were making steady progress, we were less than halfway and I suggested that I would go and get a takeaway for my workers, Roy, Andrzej and myself.

The rigging crew were catered for by their own company so we didn't have to worry about them. Andrzej accompanied me to the nearest fast food joint where we bought burgers, chips and drinks for everyone. We returned to the stifling heat of the factory to eat. By mid-afternoon we were filthy and exhausted, but we had made great headway. The flat bed truck was two thirds full and the load securely fastened. The sheer bulk of equipment that needed to be moved was enormous and slightly overwhelming. It was at 6.30pm when the truck was fully loaded that we decided it would be best to leave it along with the forklift overnight at the factory. There was a 24 hour security detail on duty, so there was no risk of any theft. We called the rigging company and requested an additional seven tonne truck to be sent the first thing the next morning. Still to be moved was the fragile cutting lathe, the mother stampers, the vast array of spare parts from the upstairs area and the scrap presses and equipment that were housed in the outdoor lock up. Dehydrated, filthy and weary, we locked the factory and headed back to the Northern suburbs. Roy and Andrzej travelled with their driver back to the lodge while I went straight home for a cold beer and a bath. Needless to say we all slept well that night.

We met at the factory the following morning at 8am, knowing we had put a big dent in the job at hand. The seven tonne truck was waiting for us and we got straight to work. Using a large hammer, we smashed the lock to the outside storage area and after many attempts with the forklift, we managed to drag the ancient presses from where they lay embedded in the soil. Once this was complete, Roy and Andrzej continued with the delicate task of dismantling the cutting lathe. The riggers had brought large wooden boxes to house the multitude of spares from the upstairs area. It was when these were slowly being brought down that Eatwell decided to show his face. He had obviously driven past and seen the loaded trucks. He stormed into the factory looking flustered and unhappy. Andrzej had noticed his arrival from the cutting room and came out to meet him as well.

"Gordon, I'm not too happy with what's going on here. You guys are taking my machines and you haven't even paid me," he moaned.

"How's it going Slade?" I said wearily. "Um, the machines aren't leaving the country just yet."

It was then that Andrzej decided to intervene.

"Look Slade, we are all grown-ups here. No-one is running away with anything. If you could send your bank details, we will arrange payment immediately."

This had a miraculously calming effect on him, and he left us in peace to continue the job. Andrzej returned to the cutting room, shaking his head. Soon enough the receptionist from Duke Box appeared with a printed sheet of paper. On it were the details of two bank accounts. One in Zimbabwe, one in the UK. The deal was the full amount less my commission to be split between the two. Andrzej immediately got onto the phone to Poland to arrange for the transfers to be done. In the meantime, our job at the factory was nearing completion. All that was left to load were the thousands of mother stampers that we piled into a large wooden box.

I had secretly hoped that they would leave these with me, but the decision was made to take them. And so every single stamper from every single record the plant had made in its history was removed from its cardboard sleeve and stuffed in the box. Although I was sad to see them go, I fared quite well from the leftovers. I walked away with a set of high quality vintage JBL speakers from the cutting room, and thousands of stiff cardboard album sleeves that were used for housing the mother stampers. I used these to ship albums all over the world for many months after. After a final look around the factory we instructed the rigging company to drive the two fully loaded trucks carefully to Speedlink Cargo in Msasa. Roy travelled in the hired vehicle with the driver while Andrzej came with me.

"I never want to see this facility again," he said under his breath.

I was in full agreement. The two cars arrived at Speedlink well before the trucks. We used this time to prime the staff and get them prepared for the imminent arrival of the trucks. A tray of tea was brought to us as we sat in the shade outside near the bay where the trucks would be offloaded. Again Roy struggled with his right hand shaking as he tried to drink his tea. It was obvious he was frustrated and embarrassed by it, but we did what we could to assist and all was well. We were almost there. Eventually the two heavily loaded trucks arrived. First to be offloaded was the seven tonne truck that carried the cutting lathe. Special care was taken with this and the workers in the factory quickly knocked up a heavy duty wooden crate with extensive padding to protect it. As this was being done, the scrap presses and other equipment were being brought in by a forklift and placed in the vast factory bay. After a while, the seven tonne truck left and the big thirty tonne flatbed was reversed into position for offloading. It must have been 4pm when the entire plant was finally safely lifted and placed in long lines in the bay. Tired but satisfied, we left Msasa to go home and wash up. Roy and Andrzej had both asked to be taken back to The Coimbra Restaurant that evening for dinner. I was in full agreement to this plan and told them I would collect them at at 6pm.

I arrived at the lodge early to find them both sitting by the pool with the owner Colin. They were discussing the two large tiger fish mounts that were placed on the wall outside the lodge to the front. Andrzej had seen the pictures in 'Beneath the Zimbabwe Sun' and was keen to try his hand at catching one. Native to the Zambezi River with giant teeth and a ferocious attitude, African Tiger Fish are dominant, terrifying predators widely regarded by many to be the most exciting freshwater game fish in Africa. There was a distinct glint in Andrzej's eye as we recounted our many experiences catching them. It was decided that if we could conclude our business in the morning at Speedlink Cargo, we would take the four hour drive to Chirundu on the Zambezi River to give it a go. We had the hired vehicle and Colin, the lodge owner, knew of a fishing camp not far from the bridge that crosses the Zambezi into Zambia.

The dinner at The Coimbra was superb as usual and our group was in good form. All that was left was the meeting with the insurance broker the following morning and we would be done. I dropped the happy guests at their lodge and headed home. It was forty five minutes later when I got a call from Andrzej. He sounded upset, and informed me there was $500 missing from his bag. He told me he thought he knew when it must have gone missing. At some stage during the day Roy and himself had left the cutting room to watch the machines get loaded onto the truck. It must have been then, having left his bag unattended, that the theft had taken place. There had been over thirteen workers in the factory at the time and any of them could have easily slipped into the cutting room to lift the cash. I told him this kind of petty theft was common and that there was nothing that could be done at that late stage. We would have to deal with it the following day.

The three of us met at Speedlink the next morning at 8.30am. It was clear that Andrzej was upset by the theft the previous day. I told him that going to the police was pretty much futile and explained that they would never actually investigate it if we did. I suggested that it might be a better idea to try and claim from his travel insurance instead. He accepted this and we went inside the factory to take a look at the plant. The workers from Speedlink had placed the giant machinery in three long rows on the floor. Thirty minutes later the insurance broker arrived to inspect the consignment. It took less than an hour for full cover to be arranged, and after another consultation with the staff from Speedlink, we left the factory for good and headed back to the lodge. Colin had arranged a packed lunch, food for dinner, fishing equipment, and boat hire. I explained to Roy and Andrzej that normally, during the summer months, I would never venture into the Zambezi Valley. It is simply too hot. October is known in Zimbabwe as suicide month, when the temperatures rise incessantly prior to the rains. But I knew how much the competitive Andrzej wanted to get himself a tiger fish and I was happy to go for the one night. With the vehicle fully packed we headed out. For the first time ever, Andrzej triumphantly announced he would be turning his phone off and would no longer have communication with Poland. It was as if a great weight had been lifted from his shoulders. All of us were excited and elated we had managed to achieve so much in such a short space of time. We had literally moved a mountain.

"Gordon, I think we deserve to drink some beers," he said quietly. I had never known Andrzej to once order alcohol. Roy and I were wholeheartedly in agreement to this plan and I made a quick stop at a bottle store where I bought 24 cans of Zimbabwe's finest Castle Lager. We happily opened the first of many cans of beer as we left the City of Harare travelling north. Our destination...the hot Zambezi Valley.

CHAPTER FIFTEEN: CHIRUNDU

The cheerful conversation flowed during the hours we drove, with Roy in the front and Andrzej in the back as usual. We stopped briefly at the Zambezi Escarpment to take in the spectacular view of the valley and the vast wilderness of Mana Pools and Chewore that spread out below us. The heat grew in intensity as we descended and when we finally reached the valley floor, the air that blasted through the open windows was similar to that from a hair dryer. We turned left when we finally arrived at the tiny, one horse border town of Chirundu. Following the directions from Colin, we eventually arrived at our fishing lodge as the sun was setting. In front of us, the mighty Zambezi River flowed from the left past an island, and on under the bridge that links Zimbabwe with Zambia. With beers in hand we removed our shirts and headed straight for the raised swimming pool in front of the lodge to cool off. The setting sun had transformed the river into a glistening burnt orange colour and, as my guests stared out in wonder at the spectacle, a family of elephants made their way across the flood plain, through the river, and onto the island.

"Well Andrzej, you said you wanted to see the real Africa. I think this is it," said Roy quietly.

"Yes. This is certainly very beautiful," he replied.

"All this because of vinyl records. Who would have thought?" I said, as I went to get three more beers from the cooler box. The three of us stayed in the pool watching the elephants until the darkness and the nocturnal sounds of the bush surrounded us. After a quick shower and a liberal application of mosquito repellent, we took a drive through the bush to Tiger Safaris to confirm our boat booking for the next morning. On the way there we almost ran into an elephant wandering the rough dirt road in the night. We arrived to find there was a mini fishing tournament on, and it took a while to find the owner and confirm that we were to expect our boat to arrive at 6am the following day. The staff at our lodge had prepared a basic meal of boerewors and steak with relish and potatoes that we washed down with red wine. Our group retired early that night as we were exhausted and the heat and booze had taken its toll. As I lay on my bed in front of the fans I battled to get to sleep. My mind was buzzing with all of the stress and tension of the previous weeks. Eventually I drifted off.

I woke with the birds at sunrise the next morning and made my way quietly up to the viewing deck. Andrzej and Roy came soon after and we sat and watched Africa slowly awaken as we drank tea. At 6am we saw a few of the boats from the fishing tournament travelling upstream for their competition. However there was no sign of ours.

"These fuckers!" said Andrzej under his breath.

"I'm sure it'll be here anytime now," I said. "They would have called me if there was a problem." This impatience was another example of how intense and competitive Andrzej was as a person. He clearly had no concept of 'Africa Time'! A few minutes later we heard the drone of a motor and in the distance under the bridge to our right, we saw our boat making its way towards our lodge. We grabbed our rods and made our way down across the flood plain to the jetty where we would board. The driver introduced himself as we loaded a cooler box with ice and soft drinks. I knew how important it was that my guests catch some fish that morning so I had a quiet word with the driver promising a good tip if we caught. We took our seats as the driver started the motor and drove us out into one of the deep channels. The motor roared and the front of the boat lifted as we gained speed and eventually got 'on the plane'. I glanced back at Roy and Andrzej to see them both grinning excitedly as we sped under the bridge heading downstream. Keeping my eyes straight ahead I purposely avoided looking at the house of Slade Eatwell on the right as we went. Our destination was the deep channels around the mouth of the Kafue River that flows in from Zambia. Many trophy tiger fish have been caught there over the years.

We passed the old pump house on the Zimbabwe side and saw numerous herds of elephant and impala as we went. Eventually the driver took us across the river towards the Zambian side before parking the boat at an island so we could bait up our rods. A large crocodile lay on the sand sunning itself a few metres away. We would be using live bait on large tiger hooks fastened to a length of steel trace wire. The steel trace was imperative as the razor sharp teeth of the tiger fish would easily slice through any fishing line, regardless of its strength. The driver quickly set up our rods and told us how we would be fishing. Each rod would be cast out and the bale arm of the reel left open to allow the bait to travel at least thirty metres from the boat. From there we would simply hold the line near the reel with our index fingers and wait for the strike.

"How will we know if there is a bite?" asked Andrzej. "If a tiger takes your bait, you will know it, boss." said the driver.

With our rods cast out, we began our first drift past the mouth of the Kafue River. The cool of the morning was rapidly wearing off and the relentless burning heat of the Zambezi Valley started coming through. Each drift lasted around twenty minutes, after which we would reel in, restart the motor and return to the top of the channel to try again. It was on our fourth attempt as we sat drifting in silence that Andrzej had his first hit.

"There is something there!" he said out loud. I spun around in my chair to see the end of his rod bending every few seconds. Instantly I began reeling in to avoid our lines crossing.

"Let him run, let him run, watch your reel," said the driver quietly. Sure enough, the line was quietly flying out as the fish ran.

"When I say, push the bale arm over, stand up, and strike hard," said the driver.

We all watched in electric anticipation until the driver finally said. "Now!"

Andrzej did exactly what he had been told, and the hook was firmly embedded in the mouth of the great fish. Instantly his rod was bent at a forty five degree angle and his reel began to scream as the fight started. There was a brief moment of pandemonium as the driver scrambled to tighten the drag on Andrzej's reel. The great fish leapt in twisting spasms from the water fifty metres from us in a desperate attempt to spit out the hook. It was to no avail. The strike had been good. This one was coming in. The fight lasted fifteen minutes with the fish making desperate jumps and runs as Andrzej drew it nearer and nearer the boat. Eventually the exhausted fish was brought alongside the boat and lifted from the water with a landing net. Thankfully, it had not swallowed the bait and had been hooked in the mouth. This meant it would be a catch and release. Weighing in at around 6kgs it was a decent trophy size fish, and a very sweaty but triumphant Andrzej held it up for photographs to be taken. Holding the fish by the tail, the driver carefully put it back into the river where after a few seconds, it shot off to fight another day. Roy and I both got a few bites that morning, but it was Andrzej who emerged victorious. He landed three tigers in total, all of which were released afterwards. For me it had been a success.

It was around 11am when the heat became unbearable. It was like being in a fucking oven.

"I think we should get off the river now, gentlemen," I said.

The party were in agreement and we sped off back upstream towards Chirundu and our lodge. After paying for the boat and tipping the driver we made our way up to the pool for a final swim. The cool water was a blessed relief from the sweltering baking sun. Afterwards we packed the vehicle, said goodbye to the staff, and headed back through the bush to the main tar road.

Forty minutes later we began our ascent out of the valley and into the relative cool above. For the next three hours on the way back to Harare, Roy and I spoke of nothing but vinyl records. I am certain there is no one alive with such in depth knowledge of the subject. We spoke of the rare old labels like Gennet, Vocalion, Victor and Okeh. He explained in minute detail the process of making records and the pitfalls therein. We discussed what made the great Columbia classical recordings SAX, SXL and ASD so special. For all of us, it was a fascinating and special afternoon.

Our time together was drawing to an end. Roy and Andrzej were due to fly out the following day and the machines were about to start their long journey to Poland. As we approached Harare, Andrzej asked if I would like to have dinner with them that evening. I agreed, and we called Colin at the lodge to organise a steak dinner and a table to be set out by the pool. We arrived in the blissful cool of a high-veld evening. Fine South African wine and beer were brought to our table as we ate. Unfortunately Andrzej's evening was spoiled as he had turned his phone on only to be confronted by a multitude of messages and work related issues. As he excused himself to attend to these, I asked Roy what it was that drove him so hard.

"He never stops, Roy," I said, exasperated. "It's crazy!"

"I know. It'll kill him if he's not careful," he replied. Roy and I finished the wine and I left, feeling shattered, to go home. After a good night's sleep, I returned to the lodge in the late morning to bid farewell to my new friends. My involvement in the project was pretty much over, barring a few small issues that I would easily deal with from Harare. At the time I was of the opinion that I would never see either of them again. For me, it was a bitter sweet moment. The adventure was over. After a quick handshake and a warm farewell, I jumped in my car and left. It was much later that day, as I reflected on the events of the past month that I decided that it wasn't over. I decided that, indeed, I would see Roy, Andrzej and the machines again. And I would do so in Poland.

CHAPTER SIXTEEN: KRAKOW

After Roy and Andrzej left Zimbabwe, I was in constant contact with them as I was required to do a few small jobs to facilitate the shipping of the machines. Speedlink Cargo had, by some miracle, managed to fit the entire plant into a forty foot shipping container. I had a bulk order of many hundreds of records from a German buyer of mine and Andrzej had kindly allowed me to put the four heavy boxes of vinyl in with the plant. He would then ship them on to Germany from Poland. I was kept abreast of the progress of the ship as it made its way from the port of Beira, Mozambique to Gdansk. It was a painfully slow process but eventually I received pictures from Andrzej on Facebook showing them triumphantly opening the container in the factory in Krakow. I know they were extremely worried about the fragile Neumann Cutting Lathe, but to the relief of everyone, the entire shipment had arrived intact and in good condition. For them began the huge task of reconditioning and reviving the plant. Something I had no doubt they would do very well.

It was early May 2016 when I learned my favourite band, Slayer were due to play the Olympia Theatre in Dublin, Ireland with

Anthrax supporting. It was an unusually small venue for two of the Big Four of thrash metal, but I decided to go anyway. I made a call to my youngest brother in the UK and asked if he would be keen to join me. He was. The concert was in mid-June so I booked myself on an Emirates flight from Harare to London for a week and had a friend of mine in Ireland secure two tickets to the gig. The plan was to take a Ryanair flight from Stansted Airport to Dublin for one night, attend the concert, return to London the following afternoon and then fly over to Krakow the next morning. I contacted Andrzej on Facebook and told him of my plans. Although taken aback at first, he was excited and more than happy for me to visit the factory in Poland.

The concert in Dublin was superb, if a little hazy, due to my consuming far too much Guinness at The Norseman pub in Temple Bar prior to the gig. Luckily my brother had arranged a late checkout at our hotel so we were able to sleep off our hangovers. Our flight back to the UK was delayed that night so we only ended up getting to sleep at around midnight. By 5am the next day I was showered and on my way to Stansted once again for my flight to Krakow. As I walked out of the arrivals area, I was met by a beaming Andrzej who welcomed me profusely and led me out to his car which was parked in the warm sunshine outside. The drive to the Takt factory took about forty minutes through the beautiful Polish countryside. Andrzej and I talked constantly as we drove for there was much to catch up on and many stories of the challenges they had faced since vinyl record production had started. As usual, he was constantly taking work-related calls from all over the world as we drove.

Eventually we arrived at a very large nondescript building set be-hind a row of trees. I was led through the reception area and into a plush and modern boardroom, where I found none other than Mr Roy Matthews sitting eating lunch. I joined him and was introduced to another English man by the name of Sean Davies. It turned out he was an internationally acclaimed audio consultant, studio designer, and authority on disc cutting lathes. He had been brought in to assist Roy in training the young apprentice engineers in the lost art of vinyl record production. It has been said that, in addition to his wealth of experience, he had also worked with none other than The Beatles.

After a good chat and some food, Roy and Mr Davies headed back to work and Andrzej came through to take me on my tour.

"Vinyl production first or last?" he asked.

"Last I think" I replied. And so began my tour of the vast Takt facility in Krakow. Sadly I was unable to take any pictures but I can say that I was blown away by what I saw. Spotlessly clean and absolutely massive, I was led to the various departments. From the high tech CD and DVD production areas to the printing and packaging departments, it was extremely impressive and I could clearly see Andrzej's work ethic shining through in each area. The entire place was a model of high tech efficiency. Finally, I was led through to the newly-commissioned vinyl record depart-ment. Roy and Sean were hard at work in the cutting room with some young apprentices, while in the main area were the newly refurbished and working presses. An incredible sight! After such a long journey, it was a privilege to see them actually working and pressing new albums flawlessly in their new and spotless environment.

Soon after, Andrzej drove me back into the beautiful city of Krakow and to a boutique hotel in the city centre. The plan was he and Roy would pick me up at 6.30pm and take me out to dinner. I rested in my room before venturing out to have a beer nearby at 5.30pm. Right on time Roy and Andrzej arrived, and we went on an impromptu tour of the beautifully preserved medieval core and Jewish quarter as we drove. True to Andrzej's style, he had chosen a very special restaurant for dinner and the three of us had a fantastic time reliving old adventures and laughing at the various mishaps we encountered along the way. After dinner, I was dropped off in the warm fading light of a summer evening in Poland. We said our goodbyes and headed our separate ways.

After another tour of the city the following day, I got my flight back to the UK and then back to Zimbabwe. I will never forget the time I spent with Roy and Andrzej. The accidents, the adventures, the laughs, the conversations and the hardships. I believe they are now producing 8 000 albums a day. A fantastic achievement. In the end, for me it wasn't really about the money. It was about the experience. And what an experience it was! I like to think that in a small way, I personally contributed to the revival of vinyl records. Even if I did so on a wing and a prayer. I know of a couple of other plants scattered around Africa, albeit in rather more dangerous countries. If anyone would like me to go and investigate these, I am willing to do so. But before you contact me I have a very important message. NO CHANCERS PLEASE!